INSIDE
SMARTPHONES

BY JENNIFER KAUL

CONTENT CONSULTANT
Yiyan Li, PhD
Assistant Professor of Physics and Engineering
Fort Lewis College

Core Library

An Imprint of Abdo Publishing

Cover image: Smartphones help people stay connected

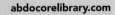

abdocorelibrary.com

Published by Abdo Publishing, a division of ABDO, PO Box 398166, Minneapolis, Minnesota 55439. Copyright © 2019 by Abdo Consulting Group, Inc. International copyrights reserved in all countries. No part of this book may be reproduced in any form without written permission from the publisher. Core Library™ is a trademark and logo of Abdo Publishing.

Printed in the United States of America, North Mankato, Minnesota
092018
012019

THIS BOOK CONTAINS
RECYCLED MATERIALS

Cover Photo: Shutterstock Images
Interior Photos: Shutterstock Images, 1, 4–5, 17, 24, 28–29, 31, 36–37; Matthew Corley/Shutterstock Images, 7; Justin Sullivan/Getty Images News/Getty Images, 10–11; Praetorian Photo/iStockphoto, 12; Avalon Studio/iStockphoto, 15, 43; Faizal Ramli/Shutterstock Images, 20–21; iStockphoto, 23, 30 (top), 34, 45; Red Line Editorial, 26, 30 (map); Nikolay Petrovich/Shutterstock Images, 30 (cell phone tower); Chee Gin Tan/iStockphoto, 30 (bottom)

Editor: Megan Ellis
Series Designer: Ryan Gale

Library of Congress Control Number: 2018949767

Publisher's Cataloging-in-Publication Data

Names: Kaul, Jennifer, author.
Title: Inside smartphones / by Jennifer Kaul.
Description: Minneapolis, Minnesota : Abdo Publishing, 2019 | Series: Inside technology | Includes online resources and index.
Identifiers: ISBN 9781532117930 (lib. bdg.) | ISBN 9781641856188 (pbk) | ISBN 9781532170799 (ebook)
Subjects: LCSH: Technological innovations--Juvenile literature. | Smart cell phones--Juvenile literature. | Cell phone equipment industry--Juvenile literature. | Cell phone services industry--Juvenile literature.
Classification: DDC 004.167--dc23

CONTENTS

THE WORLD OF SMARTPHONES

ing! A smartphone goes off in a crowded room. People look through their backpacks, purses, and pockets. They hurry to check their phones. They want to find a notification on their screen. Each person wonders who might have contacted them and why. A sound from a phone could mean many different things.

A SMARTPHONE IN ACTION

A girl checks her phone. She sees that she has received a text message. It is from one of her friends. She taps a reply on her smartphone's virtual keyboard. She adds a smiley face emoji

Smartphones allow people to do many things on the go, such as play games, write messages, and take photos.

5

REPLACED BY SMARTPHONES

Smartphones have replaced several tools people used in the past. There are apps for calculators, notebooks, maps, and cameras. People can stream movies without a television and listen to music without a radio. Many people like having one device that does all of these things. It is easier to carry around.

and hits send. Her phone dings again moments later.

The girl reads the new text. Then she closes her messaging app. She checks one social media site, then another. She opens a game she has been playing and checks her score. She scrolls through her recent photos. Then she takes a new picture and sends it to her friend.

Smartphones can do many things. They can send messages and connect people. They can run games and take pictures. But what happens inside smartphones to make all of these things possible?

Smartphones can be used for alternate reality (AR) games such as *Pokémon Go*.

WHAT ARE SMARTPHONES?

Smartphones are mobile telephones. But making calls is not all they can do. They are small, portable computers. They have advanced technology. They are connected to the internet. People can take them wherever they go.

Smartphones have hardware and software. Hardware includes the parts that make up the device. Software consists of the programs that run on the device. Together, hardware and software make smartphones work.

THE FIRST SMARTPHONE

The first smartphone was invented in 1992. It was created by IBM and BellSouth. It was called Simon. Simon had a touch screen, keyboard, calendar, and email. These functions sound basic today, but they were new and exciting at the time. Simon became available for purchase in 1994. It was priced at $1,100. Its battery lasted just an hour. It set the stage for later smartphones such as those people use today.

STRAIGHT TO THE
SOURCE

The Apple iPhone was introduced in 2007. Other smartphones at the time had keyboards with buttons. Steve Jobs was the cofounder of Apple. He believed that the iPhone would change smartphones forever. While introducing the iPhone, Jobs said:

> [Other smartphones] have these control buttons that are fixed in plastic and are the same for every application. Well, every application wants a slightly different user interface, a slightly optimized set of buttons, just for it. . . . What we're gonna do is get rid of all these buttons and just make a giant screen. . . . We're gonna use our fingers. . . . It's far more accurate than any touch display that's ever been shipped. It ignores unintended touches, it's super-smart. You can do multi-finger gestures on it.
>
> Source: Mic Wright. "The Original iPhone Announcement Annotated." *Next Web*. Next Web, September 9, 2015. Web. Accessed June 13, 2018.

What's the Big Idea?

Take a close look at this passage. What is the connection being made between the screen on an iPhone and other types of smartphones? In what way did the 2007 iPhone change smartphones? What evidence does the author present to support this idea?

iPhon

HARDWARE IN SMARTPHONES

Smartphones have many pieces that make them work. These pieces are called hardware. They are made of many materials. These include glass, plastic, and copper. Some hardware is on the outside of smartphones. Other parts are on the inside.

DISPLAYS

One part of the outside of the smartphone is its display, or screen. Smartphone displays are made of very strong glass. This keeps them from getting scratched in people's pockets. However, the glass can still break if the phone is dropped hard.

Tim Cook, the CEO of Apple, announced the iPhone X on September 12, 2017. It was the first iPhone with a screen stretching to the edges of the phone.

Broken smartphone screens can be dangerous. But the glass can often be replaced.

Layers of material under the glass make the screen a touch screen. Most smartphones use a capacitive touch screen. This type of screen stores electricity. When someone touches the screen, a small amount of electricity enters their finger. The screen notes where the electricity changed. Then it sends that location information to the phone's software. The screen can tell if someone presses, swipes, or types on the phone. But the screen does not give off electricity when something else touches it, such as fabric or a pen. A finger conducts electricity, so it works on the screen.

BUTTONS AND PORTS

Smartphones also have buttons and ports on the outside. Buttons help people use their phones. They turn on the phone, change the volume, or command the software to do something.

Ports connect phones to other devices. These include chargers and headphones. Most smartphones

CASES AND PROTECTORS

Smartphones are designed with strong hardware to keep them from breaking. However, it is still possible for a screen to crack if a phone is dropped or crushed. People can buy cases and screen protectors for their phones. Most cases snap onto the outside of a phone. Some screen protectors are made of glass. Others are made of thin plastic. Some are even waterproof. These accessories help keep a smartphone safe.

have a coating to help keep water and dust from getting into smartphones through the ports. This protects the hardware inside.

MOTHERBOARD

At the heart of the smartphone is the motherboard. A motherboard has many computer chips. These chips are made up of tiny electronic circuits. Chips send signals to each other. They work together to make the smartphone work.

The most important chip is the system on a chip (SoC). The SoC carries out the software's instructions. It lets apps run on the device. It works with the screen to show graphics. It works with the speakers to play sounds.

Smartphones also have memory chips. They are on the motherboard. Memory keeps track of programs and files that are in use. It helps keep programs open. This way, people can continue to use many apps at the same time. Someone can browse the internet, listen to music,

The motherboard inside a smartphone is very delicate. People who repair phones must be careful when handling the hardware.

and write an email all at once. The memory chips store information for a short time. When the phone turns off, the information goes away.

Storage chips are also on the motherboard. Storage is different from memory. It stores information for longer periods of time. Pictures, files, and apps are saved in the storage chips. They are kept on the phone until they are deleted. They remain even when the phone turns off. Storage is measured in units called bytes. Smartphones come with different amounts of storage. One gigabyte (GB) can be rounded to one billion bytes. Some smartphones have up to 256 GB of storage. The Asus ROG Gaming smartphone even has 512 GB of storage. That's enough to store a lot of photos, songs, videos, and apps.

AUDIO AND VISUAL

Hardware also helps people hear and see things on their smartphones. Microphones pick up what users say. Speakers allow them to hear voices, music, and other sounds from their phones.

Cameras are another important piece of hardware. They make it possible for people to take pictures and videos. A camera is a sensor chip inside the smartphone. It is light-sensitive. It turns image information into digital signals. The SoC receives the digital signals. Then it sends commands to the screen for display. Users can view and share the photos on their phones.

Smartphone cameras can capture sharp, high-quality images.

BATTERIES

By far, the battery is the largest piece of hardware inside a smartphone. It helps the phone stay charged for long periods of time. Smartphones have rechargeable batteries. They can be charged when the phone runs out of power.

Some smartphones use lithium-ion batteries. Lithium-ion batteries are built so that one side holds a positive charge and the other side holds a negative charge. When a lithium-ion battery is charging, the ions inside of it gradually move to the negative side of the battery. When the device is in use, they move to the positive side. The device must then be charged again to work.

Lithium-ion batteries are generally lighter than other types of batteries. They carry a lot of power for their size. However, they are only meant to last a few years. Another problem with lithium-ion batteries is they are sensitive to heat. They can catch fire or explode if they become too hot.

There are many ways to optimize how smartphones use power. Integrated circuits, or microchips, reduce the amount of power. Programs are designed to save time in loading and computing. The hardware and software work together to maximize battery life. They also make sure the battery does not overheat.

EXPLORE ONLINE

Chapter Two discusses lithium-ion batteries used in smartphones. The article at the website below goes into more depth on this topic. Does the article answer any of the questions you had about rechargeable batteries?

HOW DOES A LITHIUM-ION BATTERY WORK?
abdocorelibrary.com/inside-smartphones

SOFTWARE IN SMARTPHONES

Hardware alone does not make a smartphone work. These devices need software, too. Software is a set of instructions that a computer follows. It is written in programming code.

Many programming languages can be used for the software in smartphones. These are languages that humans can read. That way, developers can change the programs easily. The SoC inside a smartphone then translates the programming language into a language that computers can understand. This language is known as binary. It is made up entirely of

The Google Play Store is software that helps people download apps. Kindle is an app that lets people read e-books.

21

JAILBREAKING AND ROOTING

Many users are happy with their smartphone's software. Others want more control. Some choose to hack their phones. This process is called jailbreaking for iPhones. It is called rooting for Android phones. It allows users to access the code in their phones. They can install apps that have not been approved. However, jailbreaking and rooting smartphones come with risks. It can cause smartphones to run slower. It can also make it easier for other people to hack into them.

1s and 0s. It helps the software and hardware work together inside a smartphone.

OPERATING SYSTEM

An operating system (OS) is the most basic software on a smartphone. There are two major operating systems. Apple's OS is called iOS. It is a closed system. This means only the company's devices can use its operating system.

Only Apple devices such as iPhones and iPads use iOS. The company must approve all apps that run on a closed system.

Some apps use hardware such as the smartphone camera. People can add filters or change the color of their photos.

Another operating system is Android OS. It was developed by Android Inc. Google acquired it in 2005. It is an open system. Different types of phones can use the OS. There is more freedom in available apps. But there is no review process to approve phones and apps. Their quality can suffer as a result.

Operating systems help hardware and software work together. They also help other programs communicate with each other. They manage everything that is going on inside the phone.

USER INTERFACE AND APPS

The smartphone display shows the user interface (UI). The UI includes icons, menus, and keyboards. It helps people find, organize, and access content. People like UIs that are easy to understand. They also prefer those that are flexible and easy to use. Software designers make sure the UI looks good and runs smoothly.

People access apps through the user interface. Apps are the programs on a smartphone. Some apps are pre-installed. Apple Maps comes with iPhones. Google Maps comes with Android phones. Other apps can be downloaded from an app store. Apps allow people to use their smartphones for many purposes.

There are many different kinds of apps available for smartphones. For example, social media apps help people stay connected. They allow users to create profiles, send messages, and share photos. Games and entertainment apps are used for friendly competition and fun. There are apps used in education to help people learn

TARGETED ADVERTISEMENTS

Many developers earn money by selling space for ads inside their apps. Companies that buy advertising space try to learn about what app users buy. Then they show ads for what these people might want. Developers help these companies. They collect and sell information about users. Some apps use location services. This information tells the app the location of the smartphone user. The developers learn where people go and where they like to shop. Others use internet browsing history to see which websites people visit.

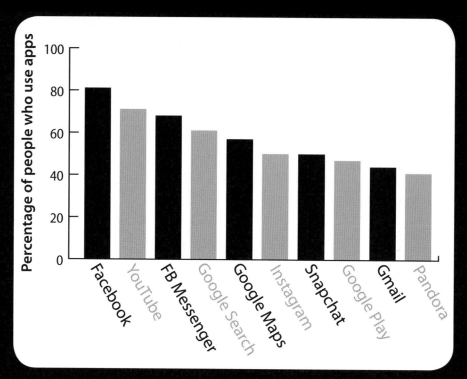

There are millions of available applications. In 2017, a company called comScore conducted a survey in the United States to analyze smartphone use. They found that over 50 percent of app users spend most of their time on a small number of applications. These include social media sites and search engines. Take a look at the diagram above. How might these apps use ads?

new things. There are apps that help people track what they eat and how often they exercise to help them improve their health. Utility apps help people function in their daily lives. These include items like calculators, alarm clocks, and calendars.

STRAIGHT TO THE
SOURCE

Technology affects how people think and feel. This often happens without people even knowing it. Tristan Harris was an employee at Google. He left Google to speak out about the control smartphones and social media have over people. In an interview with the technology magazine *Wired*, Harris explained how smartphone apps are targeting people to spend more time on their phones:

> [They] are better and better at steering what people are paying attention to, and better and better at steering what people do with their time than ever before. These are things like autoplay, which causes people to spend more time on YouTube or on Netflix. . . . YouTube has a hundred engineers who are trying to get the perfect next video to play automatically. And their techniques are only going to get more and more perfect over time, and we will have to resist the perfect.

> Source: Nicholas Thompson. "Our Minds Have Been Hijacked by Our Phones. Tristan Harris Wants to Rescue Them." *Wired*. Wired, July 26, 2017. Web. Accessed April 19, 2018.

Point of View
Harris believes smartphone apps take up too much of a user's time. Why does he think smartphones can be dangerous? Read back through this chapter. Do you agree? Why or why not?

CONNECTING AND SENSING

Smartphones are built with wireless use in mind. They let users make calls from almost anywhere. Users can browse the web and send texts. They can use wireless headphones, too. Special chips on the motherboard make all this possible. They send and receive radio signals. This lets them send information without wires.

CONNECTIVITY

Smartphones connect to wireless networks. A smartphone uses an antenna to send and

Wireless headphones such as the Apple AirPods connect to smartphones using Bluetooth.

CELLULAR
NETWORKS

Smartphones connect to a cellular network using a tower. This tower helps people make phone calls, look at images, and gather information. How does the diagram below help you understand how smartphone networks work?

1. Person A makes a phone call. The signal is received by the tower near Person A. It makes sure that Person A uses the right network.

2. The tower near Person A sends out the signal. A tower near Person B receives the signal.

3. The tower near Person B makes sure that Person B uses the right network. It then sends the signal to Person B's phone.

Smartphones connect to networks using a SIM card. These cards make sure the phones connect to the right networks.

receive signals. These signals travel as radio waves. Cell phone towers receive the signals. They transmit the signals to help people send messages, make calls, and use the internet. Cell towers are most reliable when they are a few miles away. There are many thousands of these towers all around the world to keep smartphones connected to a strong network.

Users pay to access wireless networks. One type of network is called 4G LTE. Companies such as Verizon, AT&T, and Sprint have 4G LTE networks. In 2018, 4G LTE networks had the best quality and fastest speeds. To use these networks, a phone must have the right chips.

Smartphones can also connect to the internet through Wi-Fi. This allows people to use their smartphones even in places where cell phone towers don't reach. This includes places such as airplanes and tunnels. Another wireless technology is called Bluetooth. It helps smartphones work with other devices

WI-FI HOTSPOTS

Some Wi-Fi networks are available in public spaces. These are called hotspots. They can be found in coffee shops, airports, grocery stores, and other businesses. Some hotspots are free. A user may need a password to connect to the network. Some hotspots cost money. The hotspots charge money to a user's credit card before she can access the network. Smartphones can access these networks using wireless adapters.

such as headphones and printers. Many people use it to connect their smartphones to their car speakers. This makes it possible for them to talk on the phone while keeping their hands on the steering wheel.

Near Field Communication (NFC) is a new kind of wireless technology. It helps people pay for things with their smartphones. Examples of this technology are Apple Pay and Google Pay. The phone is linked to a user's bank account or credit card. The user simply taps their phone on an NFC reader near a cash register. The payment happens automatically.

Different wireless networks are designed for different uses. They all have different ranges, signals, and types of hardware. But all networks help smartphones connect to the internet.

SENSORY INFORMATION

Smartphones have many sensors. They collect information on things such as motion, sound, and light. This helps them improve their performance.

Some smartphones can use solar energy to charge the battery. Others must be plugged in to an electric outlet.

Some sensors are on all the time. A sensor inside can warn the user if the battery is getting too hot. Others are only active when in use. The camera can adjust itself based on the amount of light entering the lens.

The accelerometer is one key sensor. It can tell the angle at which a smartphone is held. This tells the phone to change the display if the user is holding it sideways. The brightness sensor detects how much light is in the room. This tells the phone to make the screen brighter or dimmer. Another sensor can tell when the phone is close to the user's face during a phone call. This tells the phone to turn off the screen to save battery life. Smartphone sensors take in information to give the user the best experience possible.

One important sensor tells the phone where it is on the planet. It uses the Global Positioning System (GPS). The sensor receives signals from satellites that circle the Earth. The system knows where all the satellites are. It figures out which satellite each signal comes from and how long it takes the signals to arrive. Using this information, it can calculate the phone's location.

PROS AND CONS OF GPS

GPS helps people in many ways. People can follow directions to avoid getting lost. They can find smartphones that go missing. They can even find friends nearby. GPS is very accurate. It can locate smartphones within a range of a few feet. Smartphones can be found even when their location services are turned off. This causes users to have privacy concerns. Some people do not like the idea of being tracked wherever they go. They know others could study the places they go to learn their interests and daily habits.

CHAPTER FIVE

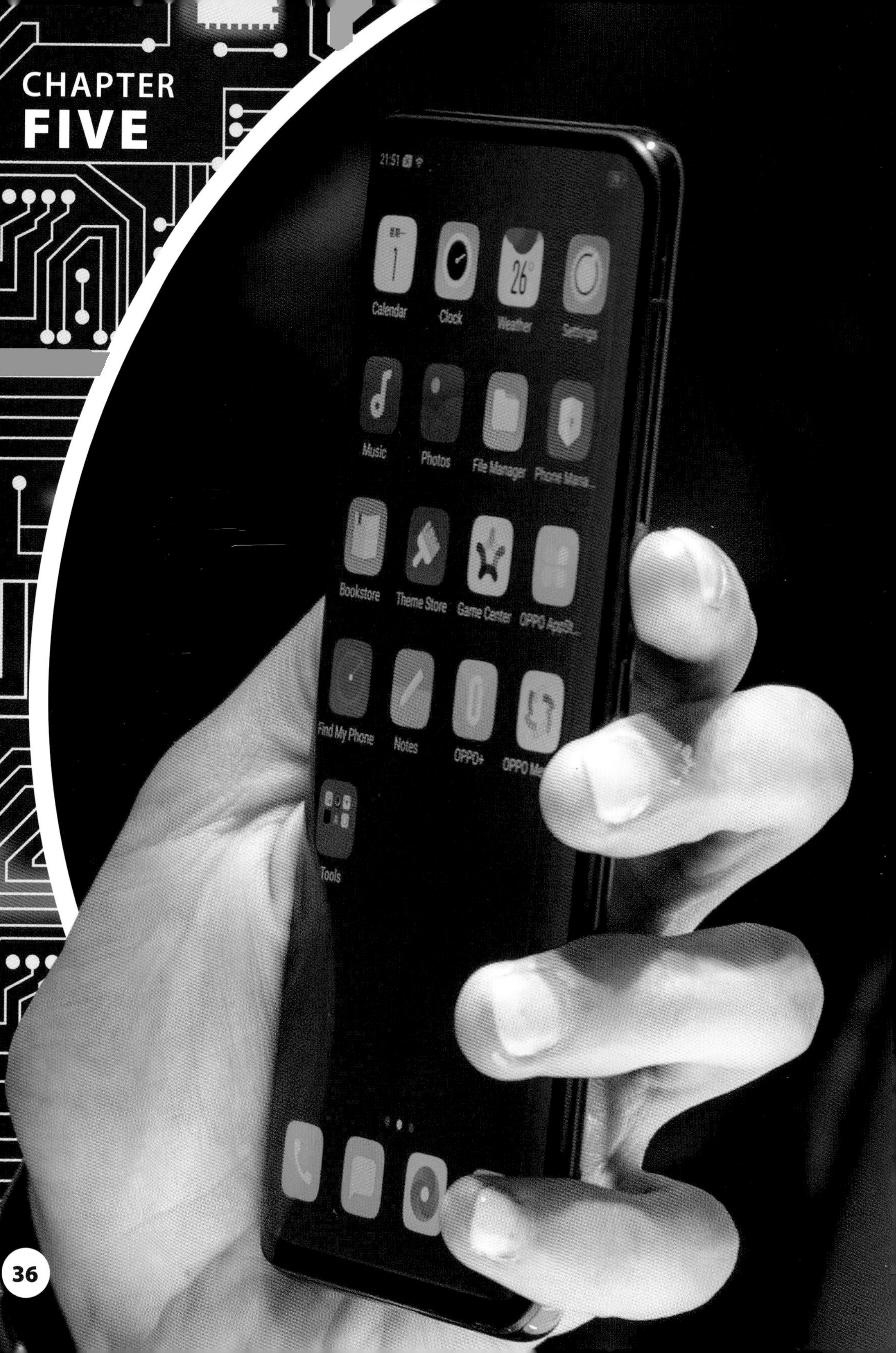

THE FUTURE OF SMARTPHONES

Smartphones are always improving. New models are released every year. There are many ways smartphones can improve in the future.

THE FUTURE OF HARDWARE

One possibility is an all-screen phone. If sensors and lenses are smaller, they could be inside. A curved smartphone design could allow the screen to wrap around the entire phone. This would allow users to interact with both sides of their smartphones.

Another area of focus is batteries. Some people want new ways for batteries to charge.

The Oppo Find X was released in Europe and Asia in 2018. It has a screen that takes up 93.8 percent of the front of the phone.

Future smartphones could be charged using tiny windmills that harness energy from the wind. They could gain their power through smartphone users' movements. Another option involves using solar power, or energy from the sun. These options could reduce the amount of electricity that smartphones need. They could limit the harmful effects smartphones have on the environment.

Moore's Law predicts the rate of improvements that will take place in technology. It suggests that the technology in devices such as smartphones will continue to become smaller and faster every year. As the technology becomes smaller and faster, it allows companies more space and freedom to add new hardware and software to their devices.

THE FUTURE OF SOFTWARE

There are many new types of software in progress. Artificial intelligence (AI) is technology that can learn and behave like humans. It is already available on many smartphones. Some examples of AI include Siri on iPhones and Google Now on Android phones. People can use AI to call family and friends. It can look up directions, play music, and more. As AI gets smarter, it will be able to do more things.

Some people are excited about AI. Others are concerned. They worry that AI technology could become more powerful. Some even think that it could harm society. Most people agree that technology is getting smarter. They are beginning to talk about what that might mean for people in the future.

Augmented reality (AR) is another newer software for smartphones. AR is technology that combines images from software with what people see in real life. A popular AR app is *Pokémon Go!* Cameras, sensors, and software work together to display Pokémon on the screen as though they are standing in front of the user. Developers use AR to create more exciting games. Art museums use AR to help visitors learn more about their art. Smartphone companies are working to improve AR. They hope to

FACIAL RECOGNITION

Facial recognition helps smartphones identify their users. It uses hardware like cameras and sensors to see what a person looks like. AI software remembers faces in the future. People can use facial recognition to unlock their phones and make purchases. It can also be used for entertainment. Users can take pictures of themselves to turn them into emojis. They can share these images with family and friends.

create multiplayer games and other experiences that can be shared among users. They want to enhance AR with images that last for longer periods of time.

Smartphones have become an important part of society. They help users learn information, find entertainment, and stay connected. Only time will tell how developers will change smartphones in the future. How smartphones change will in turn change people's lives.

FURTHER EVIDENCE

This chapter discusses possible developments in the hardware and software of smartphones. Identify one of the chapter's main points. What evidence does the author provide to support this point? The website at the link below shows potential designs for future smartphones. Read the article. Find a quote in the article to support this chapter's main point. Does this quote support the evidence found in this chapter, or does it present a new piece of evidence?

THE LEGO-LIKE DESIGN MAY END SMARTPHONE UPGRADES, REDUCE POLLUTION
abdocorelibrary.com/inside-smartphones

FAST FACTS

- Smartphones contain hardware and software that work together to perform many tasks.

- The parts that make up a device are called hardware. The programs and applications that support a device are called software.

- Touch-screen displays allow users to give instructions with their fingertips. User interfaces organize menus and applications to help users interact with their device.

- Motherboards connect pieces of hardware so they can communicate with each other, while operating systems manage software.

- Batteries give smartphones power. Lithium-ion batteries are rechargeable but only last a few years.

- Wireless networks and the GPS help users stay connected. They allow smartphones to make calls, send texts, connect to the internet, and use location services.

- Sensors gather information from smartphone users and their surroundings. They use this information to improve smartphone functions.

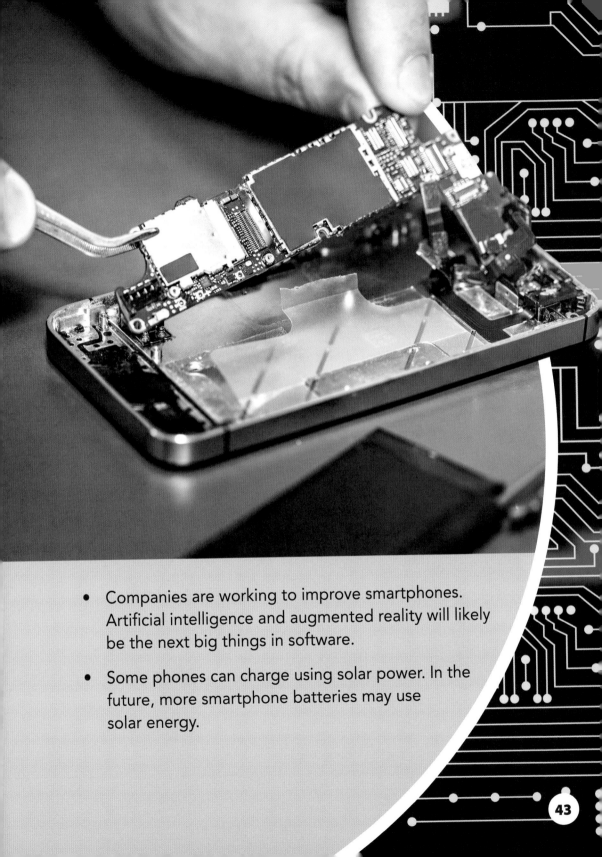

- Companies are working to improve smartphones. Artificial intelligence and augmented reality will likely be the next big things in software.

- Some phones can charge using solar power. In the future, more smartphone batteries may use solar energy.

STOP AND
THINK

Dig Deeper

After reading this book, what questions do you have about augmented reality? With an adult's help, find a few reliable sources that can help you answer your questions. Write a paragraph about what you learned.

Say What?

Studying technological devices can mean learning a lot of new vocabulary. Find five words in this book you've never heard before. Use a dictionary to find out what they mean. Then write the meanings in your own words and use each word in a new sentence.

Take a Stand

This book discusses how some developers make their money selling information about app users. Do you think this is an invasion of privacy for smartphone users? Or do you think it is a fair way for developers to make money? Why?

You Are There

Chapter Five discusses possibilities for future smartphones. Imagine you are living in the future. Write a journal entry about what the latest smartphone looks like and the things it can do. Be sure to add plenty of details to your entry.

GLOSSARY

app
a program or game that runs on a smartphone

circuit
a path through which an electric current can flow

code
symbols used to represent information

developer
a person or company that creates software

device
a piece of technology such as a smartphone

emoji
an image meant to show an emotion; also called an emoticon

Global Positioning System (GPS)
the system that uses satellites to find the location of a device

social media
apps and websites that allow people to share information with others

text message
a short message that is often in the form of typed-out text

user
someone who uses a smartphone or other device

wireless network
a system that allows people to communicate through the use of radio waves

ONLINE
RESOURCES

To learn more about smartphones, visit our free resource websites below.

Core Library
CONNECTION
FREE! COMMON CORE MULTIMEDIA RESOURCES

Visit **abdocorelibrary.com** for free Common Core resources for teachers and students, including vetted activities, multimedia, and booklinks, for deeper subject comprehension.

Booklinks
NONFICTION NETWORK
FREE! ONLINE NONFICTION RESOURCES

Visit **abdobooklinks.com** for free additional online weblinks for further learning. These links are routinely monitored and updated to provide the most current information available.

LEARN
MORE

Idzikowski, Lisa. *Computer Science in the Real World.* Minneapolis, MN: Abdo, 2016.

Ward, Lesley. *Tech World: Cell Phone Pros and Cons.* New York: Teacher Created Materials, 2018.

INDEX

About the Author

Jennifer Kaul is an author of children's and young adult literature who hopes to encourage thought, spark conversation, and make the world a better place.